Blueberries

cranberries

and lingonberries

for everyone

A handbook for gardeners

Jennifer Trehane

BLUEBERRIES, CRANBERRIES AND LINGONBERRIES FOR EVERYONE

Jennifer Trehane

Published by
Jentree Productions
Church Cottage
Hampreston
Dorset
BH21 7LX
UK

jennifer@trehane.co.uk

ISBN 978-1-899499-48-9

Distributed by The Dorset Blueberry Company
www.dorset-blueberry.co.uk

Printed in the UK by The Minster Press
14 Mill Lane, Wimborne, Dorset BH21 1LN, UK
Tel: +44 (0) 1202 882277   www.printsolutions.co.uk

Also by Jennifer Trehane

"Camellias". Their Cultivation and Use. B.T.Batsford. 1998. (out of print).

"Blueberries, Cranberries & Other Vacciniums". Timber Press. 2004.

"Camellias, The Gardener's Encyclopedia". Timber Press. 2007.

Contents

>

Introduction

Why grow blueberries ?

There is nothing better than eating your own, home grown fruit, its as fresh as it can possibly be, absolutely no "food miles".

The varieties we grow in our gardens today are highly ornamental, giving interest all year round even as young plants.

* Scented flowers in late spring.
* Fruit to pick from early July until October.
* Brilliant autumn colour.
* Young stems are red all winter.
* Easy to grow in containers.

Even very young children love blueberries – they later become adept at picking

Any disadvantages? Just that blueberry plants do take a few years to grow to maturity so those that are in a hurry may choose to buy three or four more mature plants to gain a year or three.

Some misunderstandings about the needs of cranberry plants have been exploded since it has been found that they enjoy the same conditions as blueberries, making them ideal companion plants. A small chapter is devoted to their cultivation.

We now have sufficient experience to know that, provided they are given the right conditions to start with, both blueberries and cranberries are easy to manage even in the smallest garden or city yard. This small book gives a comprehensive and easy-to-follow guide for gardeners of all levels of experience to use and, hopefully, help to gain many years of pleasure from their blueberry--- and cranberry plants.

Chapter 1. Blueberry background

What is a Blueberry ?

This is a frequently asked question. The Oxford English Dictionary tells us that it is
1. "any of several plants of the genus *Vaccinium* with small blue-black edible fruit,
sometimes cultivated. 2. the fruit of these plants".

This opens the door to a genus with a number of plants, nearly all of which enjoy acidic,
heathland types of soils. Most of the species that are actually harvested for eating are found
growing wild in Northern Hemisphere countries. There are two main groups of small fruited
blueberries, each with long histories as wild plants and devoted followers; Bilberries and
the North American lowbush blueberries. Neither is particularly suited to garden cultivation
but are mentioned here because they ARE blueberries, and important as economic crops for
the pharmaceutical industry and for processing for the catering industry. The ones grown
commercially for their fresh fruit all come from the larger bushes of the various types of
highbush blueberry.

Blueberries and health

A great deal of research has been carried out on the subject of the health benefits of
blueberries.

It has now been proved that naturally produced chemicals found in blueberries have both
age-extending and disease-preventing properties. The health-giving properties are all in the
dark colour of the skin, and in the case of the small fruited species, the flesh. The colour is
unaffected by heating.

Publicity, combined with a general trend towards "healthy eating", resulted in them being one
of the first fruits to be given the title "Superfood".

Blueberries have been used since time immemorial for medicinal purposes, with all parts of
the plant said to have their uses, from the treatment of diarrhoea, problems of menstruation,
bladder disorders, rheumatism and more. Nowadays it is the berries that are accepted as the
main providers of benefits.

The first clinical and laboratory research was carried out in the 1960's, following reports
that pilots on night-time bombing missions during WW2 reported improved night vision after
eating blueberry jam over a long period. Research, by Italian scientists in the 1980's using
bilberry/lowbush blueberry extract, reported that their trials indicated a high percentage of
patients showed improvement in short sightedness after being given daily doses of 150mg
of bilberry extract, plus vitamin A for 15 days. Higher doses over a longer period resulted in
reduction or disappearance of hemorrhages in the retina of the eyes of diabetic patients.

Since then much more research has been carried out, particularly at Tufts University in Boston,
USA, proving that blueberries do indeed have significant health-giving properties if eaten
regularly, or taken as extract or in juice. But do look at the content of most blueberry juices
sold in supermarket cartons; they may surprise you!

Anti-oxidants

Our bodies, during the course of daily life, naturally produce waste products that have to
be disposed of or neutralised. One group of waste chemicals, termed "free radicals", are
produced when the oxygen we breathe is used during its conversion into energy in the living

cells which make up our bodies. Normally, a healthy body gets rid of "free radicals", but if they are not removed efficiently the body suffers "oxidative stress" and health problems arise.

The main group of beneficial chemicals involved, and found in blueberries and other dark coloured fruit and vegetables, are complex but can be given the term "polyphenols". They act as "anti-oxidants", which mop up harmful "free radicals". There are other benefits such as boosting levels of chemicals that neutralise cancer-causing agents and repairing damaged DNA. Age-related diseases and problems such as arthritis, memory-loss and poor eyesight are also shown to be delayed in experiments using laboratory rats fed regularly with blueberry extract.

Wild blue berries

Bilberries. We may call them blaeberries, brylocks, whortleberries, wimberries, or any of the other regional names given to the wild blue berries found on, mostly, upland moors all over Britain. Or what about blabar (Sweden), bickberren (northern Germany), blauberren (Southern Germany), myrtilles (France)? They are all one species:- *Vaccinium myrtillus*.

They are found, spreading as a low growing carpet, ranging in height from about 10cm on open exposed moorland to 30-40cm or so in sheltered places under birch or other small trees.

Bilberries on the Derbyshire moors just outside Sheffield

Newly formed fruit

Ripe bilberries

Berries are very small but very tasty and have been picked by generations of families as an annual ritual, particularly on the moors of Northern England and Scotland.

They are purple all the way through. Mention fingers stained deep purple, and the give-away purple lips and mouths, and a broad smile appears on the faces of those who "always went up on the moors every August as a child, picking those berries. Mum used to make wonderful pies with them".

Picking bilberries in 1908 in Cheshire

North American lowbush blueberries

If you buy blueberry muffins from a baker the chances are that the small blueberries in them come from the USA (mostly from Maine), or from Canada (Nova Scotia). They, like the bilberry, are purple all the way through, but are another species, most often referred to as the North American wild lowbush blueberry *Vaccinium angustifolium,* harvested in great volumes, from what are technically "wild" areas, known as blueberry "barrens" because of the poor acidic soils that the early settlers found totally unproductive for ordinary farming. These plants are low growing, but slightly larger and more woody than the bilberry. Areas with a large concentration of plants are "farmed" to keep them productive, by burning off areas that have become old and straggly every few years, mowing off any emerging shrubs and small trees and even, in some areas, using herbicides to control competing weeds such as grasses.

Blueberry Hill, Maine, in the Fall

Showing a blueberry comb, used for harvesting

Individual lowbush blueberry plant

Where an area is flat and boulder-free machines are now used to harvest the berries but most "barrens" are on hillsides and have a number of boulders so harvest time is when whole families gather with their "combs" to bring the berries in to the pack-houses. Large ones for the men, medium ones for the women and small ones for the children.

They use an upward sweeping motion to take the combs through the bushes, bringing up the berries plus some leaves and bits of twig into the base of the comb. These are poured into boxes, allowing some of the dross to blow away as they fall, but most of this gets removed in the packing sheds before being sent away for freezing, ready for sale to the catering and juicing trade, or nowadays the pharmaceutical industry.

The State of Maine is the leading producer of North American lowbush blueberries. In 2009, 88.5 million pounds (American) was harvested. The value was US$32 million.
Of these 14,729 metric tons was exported as fresh fruit and 3,397MT as frozen. Japan was the top customer for the frozen berries.
The USA imported 4,449 fresh wild blueberries and 18,875 frozen wild blueberries in 2009, mostly from Canada.

In the 1860's companies in Maine started to can wild blueberries. At this time they cooked the berries in pots over a fire and filled and sealed the cans by hand. Many tons were shipped out by boat from ports along the coast. As the railways reached the region they gradually took over and by 1899 virtually all blueberry fruit was canned and transported by rail.

In the 1920's there were four canning operatives operating in Maine. In fact the Washington County Commissioner stated in 1926 that "Maine packed 70% of all commercially prepared blueberries in the United States or in the world."

Now, canning is replaced by freezing as the chosen method of preservation.

Highbush blueberries

These are our "garden" blueberries. Why use valuable space growing wild plants that are not high yielding when you can harvest several kilograms from modern, large fruiting varieties in half the area ?

All come from North American species, most are derived from wild plants of the Highbush blueberry *Vaccinium corymbosum*, found growing wild particularly in the Pine Barrens (forests) of New Jersey.

This shows the relative size of bilberry with the bigger highbush blueberry fruit

Map to show location of the Pine Forests, marked with a red dot

The "pineys", (people living in the pine barrens), hung large home-made baskets round their necks, bent the blueberry branches over them and beat them with clubs to shake the ripe blueberries off.
"Aint nothing to knock off two hundred pounds in less than a day" according to one old man.

(Above) A branch bearing fruit

(Left) A wild highbush blueberry plant in the pine forest

Growing alongside these plants are some lower growing blueberries with smaller berries; a different species, *Vaccinium pennsylvanicum.*

These are known to hybridise naturally with their taller cousins.

The understorey includes, amongst other plants, the wild, more compact blueberry Vaccinium pennsylvanicum

We can learn a lot from the conditions these plants enjoy in the wild.

Here, the soil is an acidic coarse silver sand enriched only by the rotting leaves etc from trees such as the pines, hemlocks and the shrubs, vines, and smaller plants around them.

There is plenty of fresh water, mostly less than a meter below the surface, as the whole area is criss-crossed by running fresh water streams and small rivers. Most of the wild highbush blueberries, certainly the ones with the sweetest berries, are found near the edges of the forest where they get plenty of light. The berries are smaller than our cultivated fruit, but like them, have blue skins and greenish/yellow flesh. They have shallow, very spreading root systems. Winters are cold but summers mostly dry, hot and humid.

Early cultivation

Some of the European farmers, early settlers, who made their homes in the east coastal regions of North America where blueberries are found growing wild, tried to grow them as cultivated crops. They dug wild plants up and replanted them in their gardens, but they failed because they did not understand the needs of these plants. Instead of learning from the conditions they enjoyed in their native wild habitats they treated them like the corn and potatoes they grew round their homesteads. "We'll give them a good start with plenty of muck from the cow byres". This was too much for blueberries so they curled up their toes and died.

The taming of wild blueberries—how they finally came into cultivation.

The work of the two "blueberry" pioneers Dr Frederick Coville (1867-1937) and Miss Elizabeth White (1887-1954).

Just after the turn of the 19th/20th century USDA (United States Department of Agriculture) scientist Dr Frederick Coville had begun to appreciate the potential importance of blueberries and was carrying out experiments in order to better understand their needs. Amongst his experiments he grew seedlings in glass jars in his laboratory so that he could study their root systems, and soon discovered that they were very fine and fibrous, with no microscopic root hairs like most plants. This type of root system on slow growing shrubby plants makes them vulnerable to chemical scorch from concentrated chemicals, such as those produced from the "muck" used locally by the farmers.

These results gave a proper scientific explanation for the failure of so many attempts at blueberry cultivating at the time.

His other experiments, using different types of soil, also proved that blueberries do best in the acidic, free draining "poor" soils of their native habitats.

Plants grown in suitable soil proved to have enormous, spreading, shallow root systems extending up to 1 meter from the main stem in mature bushes – useful knowledge when it comes to providing irrigation and fertiliser in cultivation. Most of the roots are found in the top 25-30cm of soil but may extend to no deeper than 60-80cm – useful again when considering sites for planting blueberries.

Dr Coville & Elizabeth White working together at Whitesbog. Photo: The Whitesbog Preservation Trust

Dr Coville had skills as a propagator and hybridiser, and some of his published work attracted the attention of cranberry grower Elizabeth White from Whitesbog, Burlington County. NJ. She had the same enterprising spirit as Dr Coville and had noticed that some of her staff were making good money by picking wild blueberries from the pine forests around her property. She also appreciated that they knew of areas where the fruit was big and/or particularly tasty and that there were other differences between these patches. She not only wondered if blueberries could be added as a second crop on her farm, but had also read reports of Dr Coville's work, and thought that there was plenty of scope for hybridisation. This was the beginning of a ground-breaking partnership that finally resulted in the multi-million dollar/pound industry we know today, and a very rewarding plant to add to our garden fruit collections too.

Dr Coville provided scientific knowledge and experience, and Elizabeth White the financial support plus the use of her land and staff. Both had plenty of enthusiasm. True pioneers!

Aluminium gauges, with holes of different sizes punched in them, were supplied to some of Elizabeth White's key staff . They were sent out into the forests with the gauges, labels with their names, and bottles of formulin (a traditional laboratory preservative), and told to mark bushes which had big berries, and to bring back bottles with some of the fruit. Subsequently those bushes that had fruit of 1.25cm diameter or more, were dug up and replanted in Miss White's garden at her house, Sunningive, at Whitesbog. They were given the surnames of their finders. No problem with Sooy, Stevenson, Adams, Harding and Dunphy, but you cannot call a blueberry either "Lemon" or "Leek" so Sam Lemon's find became "Sam" and Reuben Leek's became "Rubel".

Between 1913 and 1936 Dr Coville produced 15 named cultivars from 68,000 seedlings, basing his work on the original wild selections. It took many years to get results to the stage where plants could be sold. The first three, Cabot, Katherine and Pioneer were introduced in 1920. The last, "Dixi" which means "I am done", was named just before he died in 1937.
The partnership between these two early pioneers is responsible for the birth of an industry that only came into its own nearly 100 years after they started work together.

Breeding of blueberry varieties continues to this day, with consideration being given not only to berry size, shape and flavour, but disease resistance, growth habits of the bushes, and varieties to suit different climates of the world.

Blueberries are grown commercially and in gardens in all but the most humid tropical countries all round the world.

Blueberries arrive in England

My father, David Trehane (1908-2000), first brought blueberries to the UK in 1951 when he and three other people from Britain responded to a small note in a gardening magazine. A Methodist Minister based in British Columbia, Canada offered 100 free plants to anyone in Britain as a friendly gesture after WW2. My father's original plants consisted of varieties:- Atlantic, Concord, Jersey, Pioneer, Weymouth and Rube Leek's wild selection from the forests, Rubel. The plants thrived in the acidic sandy soil in his garden on the edge of the Dorset heathland, mulched in the traditional American manner of the time, with sawdust brought from a sawmill a few miles away.

It was soon after the first berries ripened that he discovered that the local blackbird population enjoyed blueberries as much as his family.

His first commercial acre was planted in 1957, using some of the bigger fruited, more productive varieties bred by Dr Coville. Sawdust was used as a mulch, but there were, in the early years, problems with erosion in the light, sandy soil.

Five years later it was producing sufficient fruit to start serious selling to local shops, with a recipe leaflet in each punnet, as nobody knew what these strange berries were. Birds continued to be a problem. A variety of methods was used in those early days to keep them at bay, none was particularly successful.

Since then the third generation of the family has come into the business, plantations have been extended and now cover 30 acres.

Harvesting in the first Trehane plantation 1961. Note the primitive attempts to keep birds at bay

Blueberries are no longer strange. Since the turn of the 21st century, almost 100 years after they first came into cultivation, people gradually changed from "What are those berries, they look like sloes. Are they sour ?" to now not only recognising them but even asking, "What variety is that ?"

Gardeners have not been slow to take up this trend.

American Indians noticed that the blossom end of blueberries was star shaped and believed that "the Great Spirit sent the 'star' berries down from the night of heaven", to save their children from starvation in times of famine.

Wild bears are particularly partial to wild blueberries and have been known to travel with an empty stomach from 10 to 15 miles per day to seek out a favourite blueberry patch.

Chapter 2. Understanding garden blueberries– the blueberry year

Winter

The varieties of these woody plants that we grow in our gardens are mostly deciduous, spending the winter in a state of suspended animation. This state of dormancy allows the plants to survive surprisingly low temperatures outside in normal British winters. Their young stems turn red and by this time next year's flower buds, tightly clustered together in groups and appearing at this stage as single fat buds, for winter protection.

Those varieties, such as 'Sunshine Blue', 'Legacy' and many of the other Southern highbush hybrids, that keep all or most of their leaves in winter, especially in the warmer areas, behave slightly differently. They are not quite as hardy as the deciduous plants, although, in most situations their leaves become coarser textured and may simply deepen in colour or turn a deep magenta. The flower buds that are already formed for next season are clearly visible and may be vulnerable if temperatures drop below about -5°C.

In colder situations they behave as deciduous plants and shed their leaves.

'Legacy' stems in winter

Winter protection ?

Should I bring my container grown blueberry plants, into a greenhouse/garage/shed for the winter, in case they get damaged by frost ?

This is not desirable in most British gardens although there are sometimes exceptional conditions where unusually severe winters are experienced. Where pots are frozen solid for days and nights on end, and an arctic wind is blowing this may prove too much for any plant in a container, including some blueberries.

Research, carried out over the years, has shown that blueberries actually need a winter chill: they all need a period when temperatures fall below 8ºC in order to develop their flower buds properly in the following year.

Those varieties that include species that come from the colder climates, including the hybrid "Half-high" blueberries such as 'Northcountry' and 'Northsky', from Maine in the N.E of America, need up to 1000 hours accumulated over the winter and can tolerate exceptionally low winter temperatures, down to -40ºC, when grown in the ground.

The normal garden blueberries, the deciduous Highbush varieties, need up to 700 hours and are hardy down to -12ºC.

Snow protects dormant buds

The semi-evergreen blueberry varieties, which include the "rabbit-eye" and hybrid blueberries from the Southern States of North America, such as 'Sunshine Blue' and 'Legacy' need only up to 400 hours. They are tolerant of temperatures down to about -5ºC, but at this temperature may lose both leaves and flower buds, especially if in windy/draughty situations. All these "chill hours" are easily attainable in our average British winter.

In exceptionally prolonged cold winters such that experienced in Europe in 2009-2010, damage to shoot tips of both deciduous Northern highbush and Southern highbush blueberry plants occurred where plants had failed to achieve full dormancy before winter set in. However, even plants grown in 2 litre pots outdoors in nursery beds, experienced no root damage.

A blueberry plantation in winter

Spring

As temperatures start to rise and days lengthen plants gradually start to take up water from the soil, plant hormones convert the stored starch to soluble sugars and blueberry sap becomes active again. Flower buds start to break out of their protective coats and to grow rapidly. Leaves follow. It is soon apparent that flower buds contain clusters (corymbs) of flowers.

An opening flower cluster

These begin to open from about mid-April, with the Half-highs such as Northcountry and Northblue leading the way.

The early flowering varieties produce masses of flowers because insect pollinators are relatively few and far between at this time of year, so this ensures that a good proportion of the blooms are fertilised. The sweet scent produced helps to tempt the bees too. If frost is forecast a blanket of horticultural fleece makes a good insulator to prevent damage.

'Northcountry' flowers covered with fleece

Most of the garden highbush varieties flower from the last week in April through the first two weeks in May in the south of England, later further north. The half-highs (see page 48) precede them by about two weeks.

The flowers are typical of the Heather (Ericaceous) family, bell shaped and ranging from pure white through ivory to pink according to variety.

A selection of blueberry flowers from different varieties 10ᵗʰ May 2010

Each variety produces flowers over several weeks so there are flowers at different stages of development on each bush at any given time. Those at the tip of the flower cluster develop first.

In spring the old leaves of the evergreen varieties fall as young growth replaces them.

'Legacy' with old leaves, young leaves and flower buds in early May

The sweet scent, not unlike that of wild cowslips, from a group of blueberry plants is one of those bonuses for gardeners. It is not really appreciated until you have your own blueberries. There is something very welcoming about coming up the garden path on a warm early summer evening to be greeted by the scent from a couple of blueberry bushes on either side of the back door.

The scent is from the nectar produced from the base of the petal tube, and designed to attract insects.

A handsome plant of 'Chandler' in full flower

The pink buds of 'Sunshine Blue'
open to white flowers

Pollination/flower fertilisation

Why are we often told to have two or more varieties in our gardens ?

Most blueberries are self fertile to a certain extent, but some are not and all varieties produce more and better fruit if cross-pollination between two different varieties has taken place. (*The fruit consists of tiny, almost insignificant, seeds surrounded by the soft juicy tissue that we enjoy. The more seeds that are produced by thorough fertilisation the more of this tissue is produced to surround them*).

The main pollinators are bees; hive bees and wild "bumble" bees, with the latter working longer hours and in less than ideal weather conditions.

Bee hives close to a blueberry plantation

A small species of bumble bee at work
amongst blueberry flowers

The flowers have a rather narrow entrance to the corolla, making it difficult for some bees to reach the nectar at the base of the flowers. Some cheat and take a short cut by making holes to gain easier access. This enables the bee to reach the nectar but prevents pollen being carried to the next flower. Commercial growers have found that colonies of small, non-stinging, mason bees certainly help pollination as they can climb right into the flowers. Also

A colony of mason bees in a plastic pipe

A hole in a corolla is clearly seen

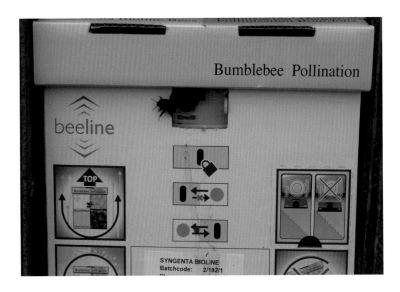

available are cardboard "hives" of a small species of bumble bees that arrive by "next day delivery" carrier, buzzing anxiously and eager to get out amongst the flowers.

As soon as flowers are fertilised the fruit begins to develop. It is at this stage, in May, that they are vulnerable to late winter frosts so it is a good idea to have the fleece handy to protect the developing berries. However, most varieties are unharmed by slight frost, only losing newly formed fruit at temperatures below -2°C.

Spring into Summer

As the flowers fade, the tiny fertilised embryo berries are soon visible at the base of them, as a small green disc, with a small black hole where the pistil (female flower part) was attached. The corolla (actually five fused petals that form a tube), turns brown and falls, leaving a scar at the top of the developing berry.

Newly formed fruit with developing leaves

If you look closely you can see the five points which remain as small insignificant features on the top of the berries, but gave rise to a native North American folk tale about the "star berries" saving the children at a time of famine.

The leaves and young shoots now grow rapidly.

Reddish in colour at first, these young shoots develop first from older growth, as short lateral branches. The more vigorous shoots come from the stronger young stems from last year's growing season. This is the first burst of growth. The second, which is when the longest strongest canes and lateral branches are produced, follows during the harvest season and continues well into late summer/early autumn and most of it matures sufficiently before winter sets in to bear flowers and, hopefully, fruit the following summer.

Next season's largest berries tend to be produced on the strongest growth from the previous year, the bulk of the crop on the smaller lateral branches, and the smallest berries from the oldest wood.

The green fruits swell, gradually turning from green to pink and by mid-summer the first berries of the early ripening varieties are beginning to show their purple/blue colour, especially if planted in a warm sunny position.

Harvesting

By the end of June or early July, provided daytime temperatures are between 16°C and 24°C, the first berries of the earliest ripening varieties are ready for picking. If daytime temperatures are below 16°C as they may be in more northern gardens, ripening will take a little longer.

Some varieties such as 'Duke' have a relatively short ripening season of about four weeks.
It is soon evident which have long ripening seasons as individual clusters carry berries of all sizes and stages of ripening.

Blueberry fruit is ready for picking when the whole berry is completely blue all over, including the part where it is attached to the fruit stalk. It should come away from the stalk easily, without tugging.
The sweetest berries are those ripened in sun and left on the bushes for a few days after they appear ripe.
The sour ones are those that are still slightly pink at the stalk end, "pinkies" in "the trade".

While plants are putting energy into developing and ripening their fruit the early shoots are becoming firm and more mature. 60-90 days after flowering, and unseen of course, they are ready to start to form next year's flower buds in the axils of their leaves.

As the ripening season progresses the plant can turn its energy to more growth and this is when the strongest shoots are produced. The longest, which may reach 1 meter or more on a well established bush, are called "canes". If these become firm enough while temperatures are still relatively high they may form flower buds for the following year. The really long ones, which may reach 1 meter on a mature bush, should be "pinched out", as with chrysanthemums, fuchsias etc, while still growing, to encourage branches to develop and make a bushier plant.

Ripe fruit of 'Duke'

'Chandler' shows berries at many stages of ripening

Some canes may reach 1 meter in height

Branches follow from healthy buds below the pinching out point

Autumn

"Season of mists and mellow fruitfulness".

For blueberries, the fruitfulness is over, apart from a possible few stragglers amongst the brightly coloured autumn leaves.

Dew sprinkled gossamer cobwebs amongst the colour

With shortening days and lowering temperatures, most garden blueberry plants, being deciduous shrubs, prepare for winter. Growth finally stops and, provided plants have not been fed too late, the tips of young shoots are firm and ready for dormancy by mid – late October.

Leaves turn golden and/or bright red. Pot grown blueberry plants make a stunning sight in the garden and commercial blueberry plantations are almost dazzling at this time of year, a sight that will last for around three weeks until the first frosts or gales blow the leaves off.

Bushes in October turn brilliant gold and red

Very late berries amongst red leaves in October

Blueberries grown in containers suddenly stop asking for water, usually around the end of October in the UK. The sap, the dilute solution of sugars manufactured in the leaves and, during the active season, used to nourish the whole plant, is no longer circulating. It has, with the help of plant hormones, been turned to starch, which is stored just under the bark in the cambium cells.

Roots become mere anchors, no longer required for uptake of water and minerals from the soil.

Flower buds, though just visible, are tightly clustered and protected by their tough bud scales, and next year's growth buds, smaller and similarly protected,

Deciduous blueberry plants are, to all intents and purposes, dormant and ready for winter.

Chapter 3. Establishment in the garden

In the ground

There are few shrubs that give as much as blueberries, both as fruiting bushes and as ornamental plants. Pruned regularly and in suitable soil on a suitable site they will be productive for at least 70 years.

They are very much "outdoor" plants, much tougher than most people realize. They should certainly not be brought into centrally heated homes or conservatories. Only the smallest plants, less than two years old, need cold greenhouse or cold-frame winter protection, although some growers do use well ventilated polytunnels. These are partly for winter protection if in the coldest regions, but are more usually used to encourage early ripening to catch higher prices for their crops, and easier picking in all weathers.

Climate and site

Many gardens have a variety of climates within them, microclimates. We have all heard the terms "that's a cold spot", or "its roasting hot there in summer".
Blueberries thrive best when given a "warm spot", where the fruit will have better flavour as the warmth from the sun will increase the sugar content. The wonderful autumn colours will be better too. A sloping, south facing site is ideal, but not essential. Semi-shade is second best but still acceptable. Heavy shade will result in spindly bushes with small berries that either fail to ripen fully, especially the "late" varieties, or taste sour.

The occasional cold winter winds, or draughty situations where the wind whistles round corners, do little damage to the deciduous blueberries, but even they will suffer if given this treatment over a long period while frozen. When subjected to biting winds while frozen some or all of next year's flower buds may be lost. The evergreen or semi-evergreen varieties certainly need a more sheltered site.

Late spring frost may be a problem for varieties that bloom early so the choice of varieties is important here.

Soil

Those who have well drained, acidic soils suitable for growing other ericaceous plants such as heathers, azaleas and rhododendrons, and a sunny site, are lucky indeed and can grow blueberries out in the garden.

The use of a meter or colour kit to measure acidity and alkalinity, (pH), helps here. The ideal range of pH4.5 to pH5.5 is just that, an ideal. It has been found that blueberries do well in light, easy to cultivate soils, pH6 to 6.2, especially if suitable organic matter is present.

pH meter indicating suitably acidic soil

What they do not enjoy is a heavy clay or clay-loam which their fine, fibrous roots find hard to penetrate and which is usually poorly drained and lacking in air. They will certainly not thrive in alkaline soils such as those with a high percentage of chalk. In these soils the minerals they need for healthy growth and fruiting are chemically "locked up" and unavailable to them so they become yellow and stunted and usually die within a couple of years.

Some form of protection from birds will be necessary when the fruit begins to show signs of colour.

When to plant

If buying plants in 2 litre pots or larger, blueberries may be planted at any time of the year. Smaller or younger blueberries are best planted out in spring or potted into slightly larger containers (see page 35), for another year.

Many people favour planting their larger blueberries before winter sets in, while roots are still active, to allow them to become established while the soil is still warm. They will be ready for immediate action when the weather warms up again in spring. Planting throughout winter is fine as long as the ground does not get water-logged. They can usually tolerate frozen roots, especially in the ground.
Spring is another favoured time as plants soon send out roots and grow quickly once the soil warms up. Even planting in mid-summer is acceptable provided plenty of water is available during this time of peak activity.

Ground preparation

Having decided on a site for planting, and checked to make sure it is not too alkaline, the soil needs to be prepared. Allow about one meter between each plant to give plenty of room for future growth. This may look generous, especially in a small garden, but cranberries or lingonberries may be planted as ground cover; a useful crop to occupy the space.

All perennial weeds need to be removed and the ground dug over to a spade's depth. Well rotted organic matter such as bark chippings especially if from coniferous trees, and/or peat, should be forked in to provide a suitable texture and future nourishment.

Rotted & incompletely rotted material, plus pine litter

Rotting pine needles gathered from under pine trees provide the nearest thing to the native organic matter blueberries receive in the wild.

Home-made garden compost may contain undesirable material for acid loving plants, especially if it contains egg shells and it may be veering towards alkaline.

Do not use animal based compost such as stable litter, "poo pickings" from pony fields, or farmyard manure, they may damage young blueberry roots.

If the site tends to be poorly drained in winter small ridges or mounds may be created for the plants in order to keep roots above winter water levels.

Planting

Make sure the prepared ground is firm, then dig out a hole for each plant.

Ensure the soil in the pots is well soaked just before planting.

Remove the pots. If root systems are "pot-bound" they may need to be freed to allow the inner roots, that are responsible for taking up most of the water and minerals, to escape. It is easy to tease the roots out with the fingers in most cases, provided they are wet and easy to work with. It doesn't matter if roots are broken at this stage.

This root system is tending to be pot-bound

Older roots are teased out

If particularly pot-bound an old carving knife is useful, to cut away the outer layer of compacted roots.

Cutting roots

Place the plant, cover the roots with the surrounding soil and firm it around the root system. The result should be a blueberry plant in the ground at the same depth that it was in its pot.

Mulch to a depth of at least 10cm, keeping the mulch out of contact with the bark of the plants if possible.

Some of this bark is not fully rotted

Chapter 4. Aftercare

Mulching

This has become more and more important as the availability of water for our gardens becomes less and less. A 10-15cm layer of sawdust was traditionally used for blueberries, but nowadays wood chippings or shreddings are used instead. This reduces evaporation from the soil, acts as an insulator that keeps root systems at a relatively even temperature, particularly on sandy soils that can quickly become very hot in summer and very cold in winter. Mulching also reduces invasion by weed seedlings. Well rotted mulching material is able to release its useful minerals for plants in the first summer.

If still only partially rotted, some extra fertiliser with high nitrogen content may be needed, specifically to provide minerals for the "rotting" bacteria that need them for their own action. In the wild the rotting process on the forest floor is gradual and the levels of fungi and bacteria breaking down the leaves and twigs are able to keep fairly constant and in balance. However, when an incompletely rotted mulch is applied artificially there is a sudden need for bacterial action and the minerals they need to do their job are in high demand. They will quickly deprive plants of these nutrients, causing yellow leaves and stunted growth.

Plant showing the yellow leaves that indicate nitrogen deficiency

Watering

All plants need water for all their life functions and blueberries are no exception. It is, in the first place, needed to bring vital minerals up from the soil, then to carry them round the plant. It is also needed for food manufacture (photosynthesis) in the leaves and to circulate to all parts from there. Demand is high in summer when the plants are most active and falls to nothing in winter when they are dormant.

As ericaceous plants blueberries would naturally prefer acidic, lime-free water. Rainwater provides this and those with sufficient water butts or tanks that collect rainwater can usually provide their plants with enough for most or all of the summer. Many keen gardeners are buying more water storage to make the most of the rainwater so freely available in winter.

A frequently asked question is, "Can I use tap water, even if known to be alkaline and possibly heavily dosed with chlorine for my blueberry plants ? "

The answer is "Yes, even if alkaline, it is better to use it than to deprive plants of water."

This is, in most summers in the British climate, only a temporary measure as rain will, before too long, dilute the chemical effect and, being naturally slightly acidic, restore desirable soil conditions again.

Mulched plants, in the garden, planted in well prepared soil with plenty of plant originated organic matter incorporated, may need no added water throughout the summer. If the soil under the mulch regularly becomes dry it should be watered thoroughly then left until it becomes dry again.

Fertiliser

Old, well established blueberry plants planted out in the garden usually need no added fertiliser if they have sufficient organic matter provided by mulch from which to draw nutrients. Younger plants may need more of a boost.

Those fertilisers formulated for quick growing plants like most vegetables and cut flowers are unsuitable for relatively slow growing shrubby plants like blueberries. These need more gentle feeding, with slow acting, less strong fertilisers. Those designed for fellow "ericaceous" plants like rhododendrons and azaleas are ideal.

The relatively recent introduction of slow–release fertilisers for garden use has been a great step forward.

Slow-release fertiliser pellets consist of a carefully formulated mixture of minerals enclosed by a polymer coating that gradually breaks down in warm moist conditions, slowly setting free the minerals inside. They are often multi-coloured to indicate the range of different minerals, the main ones providing nitrogen, phosphate and potash, with smaller amounts of lesser elements including iron and magnesium.

The release coincides with the time when the plants need the minerals for growth. Release stops when temperatures drop and plants stop growing and prepare for winter.

Just one application of the pellets over the root system as the first buds break open in spring is recommended.

A light covering of compost hides the colourful pellets from playful birds and keeps them moist. They will usually last all summer, although most of these pellets are only designed to last for 6-8 weeks. Later, if plants show signs of hunger by beginning to look slightly yellow and lacking vigour, a second application can be made no later than the end of July.

Some gardeners use liquid fertilisers and are able to choose those that are formulated for ericaceous plants. It is very important to measure the dose very carefully and to avoid overfeeding blueberries as they can become very vigorous and lush, producing excessive growth at the expense of summer flower bud formation for the following year. Feeding should stop in August to allow plants to "harden up" and prepare for winter. If still "soft" as winter arrives young shoot tips will not only be killed by frost but are also prone to fungal diseases which can spread down the stems and affect future growth and crops.

Those gardeners who stick strictly to "organic" principles have a slight problem because the usual fertilisers used are animal based, such as chicken manure pellets or farmyard manure and these can kill young blueberry plants. Blood, fish and bone, applied at a fraction of the usual rate and only when the plants are actively growing, is probably the best solution. Older blueberry plants with more robust root systems are a little more tolerant.

Protection from predators

Unfortunately we humans are not the only animals to appreciate blueberries. In country gardens near woodland deer enjoy the leaves and sometimes damage taller stems by rubbing their antlers on them.

Badgers will pull down branches to reach the berries.

Rabbits will dine on the leaves and young growth of smaller plants.

Deer damage

Badger damage

However, in both country and urban gardens, the main problem is the fruit-eating bird population; pigeons, blackbirds and thrushes are especially fond of most soft fruit and blueberries are no exception.

A netting fruit cage is the ideal solution, but if this is not possible, individual wire cages such as are used in public parks for newly planted trees, are useful for the deer, rabbits and badgers. Temporary structures supporting nylon netting are often made to keep birds at bay during the ripening season.

Bird netting over a commercial plantation

Timing is important; protection is needed before the fruit begins to turn pink as a determined blackbird will make every effort to reach the fruit once it has had a taste of even these unripe berries.

On a much smaller scale a temporary structure can be made using bamboo canes and some predator netting from the local garden centre, making sure to tie the netting securely round the tub.

Chapter 5. Blueberries in containers

"Ornamental plants, delicious fruit on the doorstep. What more could anyone want?"

Relatively few people have suitable soil, or even the space, to plant blueberries in their gardens. The majority grow their blueberries in containers and even some commercial growers use this system, albeit with sophisticated irrigation and "fertigation" systems.
In containers, with their roots restricted, the life of a blueberry plant is shorter than in the ground; about 15-20 years in tubs, more in raised beds.

Containers include raised beds, tubs, pots and troughs and, for some of the more thrifty or eccentric among us, a whole variety of other vessels including old baths and dustbins. All need to provide good drainage and, in the case of concrete or metal, to be lined with heavy duty polythene, to prevent contamination from the effects of acidic soil water that inevitably seeps from acidic (ericaceous) composts, and may cause harmful chemicals to be released from the container.

I know of one London enthusiast who grows 20 plants in tubs on his roof-top garden in Chelsea. He harvests enough fruit for his own and his family needs, including plenty for the freezer, plus some for the local shop. His bushes are active and productive for up to 15 years before they need replacing with younger bushes.
Others, particularly those with small gardens or courtyards, grow their blueberries in attractive containers and use them as ornamental features with the added, and important bonus of their fruit.

Three plants of 'Northcountry' in a wooden trough. Spring.

Compost for all containers

Compost for ericaceous plants grown in containers has to provide a free draining acidic base. Traditionally, bags chosen from a range of available ericaceous composts were used. These were made almost entirely of dark moss peat, rather finely milled, with enough fertiliser added to give nutrients for about four weeks. Not only has peat become a "no no" medium because of environmental concerns, but this type of compost quickly becomes compacted and forms a solid mass that the fine roots of blueberry plants find hard to penetrate. They also suffer from the lack of air around them, and usually rot.
At present it is accepted that ericaceous plants need some peat as it provides a group of soil fungi that form a beneficial, mycorrhizal, association with the roots, which helps their long term survival.

Soil scientists continue to work to produce a genuinely viable alternative.

My own, not very scientific experiments, and lessons learned indicate that coniferous wood chippings, ground to a mixture of fine and medium milled grades and composted for at least a year, provide a good compost, with just 25% peat in the mix.

British compost manufacturers are now bringing similar composts onto the market.

Home produced compost and "soil conditioning" compost, (mostly made from garden waste collected from municipal skips, and now readily available from garden stores), is very variable both in terms of acidity and content. We don't know exactly what has been used in these composts.

Some is excellent and I still have blueberries, azaleas, rhododendrons and heathers growing quite happily in one bed filled entirely with one purchase. However, blueberries in another bed, using the same brand but bought on another occasion, failed to thrive. It is thought that some garden herbaceous plants and shrubs included in these composts actually produce chemicals that are toxic to ericaceous plants.

Two ornamental beds, the one on the foreground made from flint blocks sourced in Dorset

Three plants of 'Northcountry' in a wooden trough. Autumn.

Raised beds

Alkaline, chalky soils provide the worst possible environment for blueberries and other ericaceous plants, but raised beds make growing them possible. Also, those with heavy clay soil that tends to be water-logged in winter, or with any other problem that makes growing blueberries in the garden difficult, find them invaluable.

Those with allotments, or enough space in their allotted fruit and vegetable plots in the garden, often construct raised beds and enjoy good crops.

Raised beds are the nearest thing to growing blueberries naturally in the garden. After the initial investment in materials and compost, and, it has to be said, hard work, raised beds are easy to maintain.

Blueberry plants, with their large shallow root systems, can spread relatively freely and quickly grow bigger, thus providing more fruit.

Holidays away in hot summer weather do not leave the kindly neighbour such a big responsibility for watering as happens with individual containers.

Materials needed :- Bricks, breeze blocks, flint blocks, decking boards, railway sleepers. Heavy duty black plastic, or pond liner. Acid compost.

Some beds are quite imaginative and attractive, worthy of a space in an ornamental garden, especially if the blueberry plants are underplanted with trailing cranberries or attractive, evergreen lingonberries.

Most gardeners using "treated" wooden decking or planks line their raised beds with heavy duty black polythene, or if possible pond liner, this prevents seepage between the boards all round which can cause unattractive discolouration and may shorten the life of the bed. Drainage holes are provided in positions that suit the site and choice of the owner.

The depth needed for blueberries is usually about 45cm. as they are shallow rooted plants, but can be more by including deeper excavations than the retaining wall, especially in well drained soils that are not actually alkaline. A lined bed is essential when the underlying soil is tested and proves to be alkaline as the ground water from such a soil will seep both laterally and upwards into an unprotected bed. If excavations are made below the natural soil level, drainage holes should be at least 10cm above this level.

Beds should be filled with the chosen ericaceous compost so that it is level with the brim after being firmed down. This allows for the inevitable shrinkage that happens when the organic matter naturally decays, and delays by a year or two the need to "top up" with more compost. Coarse bark shreddings or chippings, (not those chemically treated which can give off harmful fumes), are often used as a mulch to reduce weed seed germination and water evaporation from the soil.

Pots, tubs and other containers

Blueberries grown partly for their ornamental value need attractive pots and tubs to complete the picture.

These plants take up to eight years to reach maturity, but give pleasure over the years, not only by producing gradually increasing crops as the years go by but by looking attractive in different ways as the seasons change.

They are more manageable in containers, less likely to be over-vigorous and, since the need to produce good crops is also balanced by the need to pay attention to their appearance, likely to have more care. Please do NOT overdo this care though.

Blueberry plants have been "killed by kindness". Overwatering is the main reason. Over-feeding, especially by using fertilisers more suitable for quick growing vegetable crops or continuing to give liquid feeds when the plants are slowing down and preparing for winter is the second main cause. A more violent end is the fate of plants brought into a centrally heated house. These plants usually die as soon as growth starts.

Potting

Blueberry plants are usually bought in 2 litre or 4 litre pots and they should have well established but not unduly overcrowded root systems. Early spring potting is recommended, whatever time of year plants are bought.

Move plants up into pots about two sizes larger than the existing pot size. Over-potting, moving small plants with small root systems into big containers, is not recommended, especially in autumn/winter. Not only do the plants look swamped by their surroundings but their roots will be swamped by sour compost with static over-acidic water unmoved by the circulation usually caused by the "pull" of roots taking it up.

A young plant of 'Bluetta' bought in a 3 litre pot and moved up into a suitable ornamental pot

Over the years, as root systems fill the pots, and ever more frequent watering is needed as the water holding compost is crowded out, the plants will need moving, step by step, into bigger containers, choosing those that are wider rather than deeper, to suit the shallow root systems of blueberries.

There is a wide choice of containers available in the garden stores, ranging from wood, plastic, and a big range of pottery and ceramics. If choosing the latter two it is worth checking to make sure they are frost-proof as they will be outside in all weathers all winter.

Good drainage is essential and may involve some drilling at home. Choose an acidic compost (see page 35), If using a light-weight container include some horticultural grit, obtainable from most garden stores, to give ballast to reduce the risk of the plant falling over in wind. Water retaining gels are very useful. Mixed according to the instructions on the tub and incorporated into the compost ahead of potting they are very effective at reducing evaporation and therefore the frequency of the need to add water. Check that the roots are not overcrowded by teasing out or cutting if necessary.

Siting tubs and pots

One of the benefits of growing blueberries in tubs and pots is that they can be moved around, at least until they get too big to lift, This is when the help of wheeled trolleys is useful.

Some people enjoy their plants as attractive features within sight of the house then move them to join their other soft fruit in a permanent fruit cage if they have one, once the flowers are pollinated and berries start to swell.

Others, especially with gardens that experience very hostile winter conditions, feel happy keeping their tubs in a sheltered and possibly shady part of the garden, or even in an unheated shed or garage during the winter. They then move them into a sunnier position.

On the allotment

Well established allotments are usually geared to grow vegetable and soft fruit crops that enjoy "good" soil that has probably been enriched with plenty of manure and fertiliser over the years and is not sufficiently acidic for blueberries, pH6.2 or less, probably being either neutral (pH7) or slightly alkaline.

Raised beds are the obvious answer. Pots, tubs and other containers need more attention, especially to watering in summer when both time and supply is often short and even rationed. Some people manage to reduce the need for watering containers by burying them up to their necks in the soil.

Watering

Water supply has already been mentioned, (page 31). Of course plants in pots and tubs need more attention than those in the garden or in raised beds, and especially if they are in full sun.

Water thoroughly, when the plants need it, not as part of a lifestyle routine. It is surprising how often wilted leaves are seen on plants that have "been watered every day". Many have wet compost in the top 5-10cm., but are bone dry below this level.

Feeding

Use the same ericaceous fertilisers as are used in the garden, but in proportion to the size of the container container and following the instructions on the packet.

Chapter 6. Routine care for all

Weed control is obviously necessary, not only to remove competition for air, water and nutrients from the blueberry plants, but to keep weed seeds from contaminating the crop; it is quite difficult to extract thistledown from clusters of blueberries.

Watering during the growing season is essential for container grown plants and may be needed for those planted in the garden, especially if not mulched.

Pruning

Blueberry plants are slow to establish and to reach maturity, but those in good soil conditions with plenty of room for roots to spread can live for at least a human lifetime. Pruning is a key factor in keeping blueberries productive over a long period.

Understanding the annual pattern of growth certainly helps most gardeners when deciding what and when to cut their blueberries. (See Chapter 2)
Most newly purchased young plants need little or no pruning in the first year. Thereafter pruning becomes more important for two reasons:- 1. To control and shape the plant. 2. To stimulate annual growth and keep the plant productive, giving regular crops of good sized berries for many years to come.

The aim is to have a mixture of young, middle-aged and older wood, the last being a support system for the first.

Winter pruning

This is traditionally a "New Year" job in commercial plantations, when plants are fully dormant, the leaves have fallen and it is possible to see what needs to be cut out.

Pruning in the snow

Smaller plants should have old, twiggy growth that has already produced fruit and will no longer be unproductive removed. Branches that are overcrowded or will touch the ground should also be cut out. This should leave a good framework for the future. Sometimes pruning is necessary in early Spring. Provided it is done before the main flush of growth starts this is acceptable :-

Young plant ready for its first pruning   *After pruning, with removed twigs on ground*

A slightly older plant showing old wood being cut out

A mature plant which has had some old unproductive branches cut to ground level, resulting in young cane growth

A chain saw was used on this bush, leaving a stump. Regrowth has followed in summer.

The same principal applies to older bushes, with some of the older branches which have by this time produced a grey flaky bark, removed either at ground level or cut back to a strong, younger fresh looking red coloured branch.

Tall strong young canes can have the top third cut back, making sure there are viable buds on the stem behind the cut, ready to break out into new branches in the following summer.

Young plants may arrive in spring with long "leggy" stems that will produce tall plants. If cut back they will quickly grow into a more compact bushy shape.

'Duke' pruned in mid-April

'Duke' growing well 30th May

'Duke' pruned hard in April and now growing into a much more compact plant

Summer pruning

This is done to control height and encourage branching lower down, which not only keeps fruit within comfortable reach but also prevents heavy crops of fruit on long young canes falling to ground level.

Canes of 'Bluecrop', if not reduced in length, will flop down when carrying a heavy crop

It involves pinching out the tips of the vigorous canes as they become firm. If done soon enough branching will take place in the current year although this may not be mature enough to produce flower buds for next season.

Tall cane

New shoots

Fruit thinning

Fruit demands a lot of energy from a plant. To both swell and ripen crops a good balance of leaves is needed to produce the necessary nutrition.

Some varieties set more fruit than the plants can comfortably support and it is not unknown for them to collapse and die as a result of being over-burdened in this way.

Overcropping

Reducing the number of berries by up to a half, just after they have formed, may be vital for survival. This will encourage new growth within a few weeks, and not only will the plant be saved but remaining berries should be larger.

Chapter 7. Blueberry Varieties

Recent work by hybridists has resulted in a much wider choice of blueberry varieties to enable commercial growers and gardeners, who live in parts of the world with extremes of climate, to produce reliable crops of fruit. We now have varieties suitable for those who experience exceptionally severe winters and also for those who have hot dry summers.

Blueberries for cold climates

For those living in the areas of northern America, northern Britain and parts of Europe and Scandinavia, where winters are long and cold, often with heavy snowfall, the northern highbush blueberry varieties may not always be rewarding. Their origins are in the relatively sheltered forests typical of New Jersey. In more exposed situations they are prone to having branches broken by heavy snow, and sometimes suffer from "bark-split" and other damage in winter. In addition, although summers are often quite hot and with long days, they are relatively short, so many of the mid-season to late ripening highbush varieties fail to ripen fully in some years.

This is where the North American lowbush blueberries come into the picture as they originate from Maine and Nova Scotia. They thrive on exposed open land where winters are long and harsh, with temperatures going down to -40ºF, and heavy snowfall is accepted as normal. As their name implies they are low growing, wind resistant, and are also quickly blanketed with insulating layers of snow in winter. With fine twiggy stems and compact habits they are physically suited to their conditions. These include short, often hot, summers so they break dormancy and burst into flower quickly once temperatures rise in the spring. The berries ripen over a short period in summer.

Their early flowering can be a disadvantage in warmer regions as flowers are prone to damage from late spring frosts if not protected and there may be a shortage of pollinating insects at this time.

Selections from particularly fruitful wild lowbush colonies have been made, named, and introduced to cultivation in North America and more recently in Europe. 'Putte' is a particularly successful Swedish introduction. These varieties have small fruit that is purple/blue throughout and the sweet intense flavour associated with the species. They have also been used by hybridists as parents to cross with other highbush species to produce a range of exceptionally hardy half-high varieties. These have variable characteristics depending on the proportion of highbush and lowbush genes in their parentage.

Warm climates

Areas that experience long hot, dry summers, where temperatures regularly rise to 40ºC or more, experience different problems when growing northern highbush blueberries. The fruit of many varieties tends to shrivel as moisture is drawn out more quickly than it is replaced from the roots. Skins become thicker and therefore tougher which is not a desirable characteristic. Like many plants that originate in or on the edges of forests, leaves are relatively thin and lose water by transpiration relatively quickly.

The wild highbush species *Vaccinium asheii*, or Rabbiteye blueberry, from the warm south eastern States of North America is adapted to the hot summer temperatures and poor dry soils of the more exposed areas where it is found. It tends to have a root system that penetrates deeper into the soil than its northern relative and has relatively tough leaves that do not lose water so readily.

Varieties of the rabbiteye blueberry have been cultivated commercially in warmer parts of America, New Zealand and Australia for many years and some of the fruit from this species still finds its way onto our supermarket shelves. It has never become popular with gardeners.

However, its genes have proved of great value to hybridists. They have crossed chosen varieties of rabbiteye blueberries with selected varieties of northern highbush to produce a group of hybrids collectively known as Southern Highbush blueberries. These combine the heat tolerance of the rabbiteye with the superior fruit quality of the northern highbush.
Many of these new hybrids also include another heat tolerant species, *Vaccinium darrowii* that is evergreen so many of the Southern highbush varieties have this characteristic.

This group of blueberries now allows both commercial growers and home gardeners to produce high quality fruit of excellent flavour in hot climates.

Although bred for hot climates it has been found that most varieties grow and produce good crops in a surprisingly wide range of cooler, but not cold, climatic conditions. "They grow well from San Diego to Seattle" is an often quoted saying.

Gardeners are also finding that the ornamental value of some of these hybrids is a major attraction.

'Misty'has the attractive grey/green leaves
of many of the Southern highbush hybrids

'Sunshine Blue'on May 31st, showing its ornamental
blue/green foliage contrasting well with
its flowers and bronze young growth

Variety list

Although listed in alphabetical order the key below indicates three groups of blueberries :-

Northern highbush (NHB) blueberries are most widely grown mainly for their crops of fruit. The bushes, although slow to come to maturity, grow into substantial bushes capable of bearing crops of 2-4Kg. Their ornamental appeal, although often much valued, is of secondary importance. The majority of the varieties listed are suitable for the climates of all but the coldest areas of The British Isles, but even in these there are often suitable places that have more benign microclimates where such blueberries thrive.

Southern highbush hybrids (SHB) vary greatly in habit and eventual size. They are a little less hardy and may suffer damage to flower buds in the colder winters. Otherwise many varieties are both high yielding and have very visually attractive growth habits, and the grey/green, often evergreen leaves, with colourful young growth in spring are an added attraction.

Half-high blueberries (HH) are useful additions to gardens where either their small berries are preferred to bigger berries for eating, or their exceptional hardiness is valued. An attractive, low growing habit makes them useful for planting at the front of a border or raised bed, often associated with highbush varieties behind them and cranberries in front.

This habit also makes them attractive for smaller pots in smaller garden areas.

'Northsky' bearing fruit.... A similar plant a few months later with its autumn colour

Vaccinium asheii is known as the rabbit-eye blueberry, apparently because the pink spot that forms at the calyx end of the berries where the flower was attached as the fruit starts to ripen resembles the pink eye of a rabbit.

The name "Huckleberry" confuses many. The American huckleberry, made famous by Mark Twain, is, depending on the customary name in each region, either from the same genus, Vaccinium, as the blueberries or from another genus from the same family, Gaylussacia. They are usually blue/black but the Red Huckleberry is, as its name implies, red :- Vaccinium parvifolium.

In Britain the "Garden huckleberry" is sold as seed. It is actually from the unrelated genus, Solanum, which also includes tomatoes, potatoes--- and nightshade. This "huckleberry" is semi-tropical and is treated as a half hardy annual, like tomatoes. Although not poisonous it should not be eaten until fully ripe in mid-late September.

Varieties

In the following alphabetical list NHB indicates Northern highbush, SHB Southern highbush, and HH Half-high.

Early season indicates ripening from approximately early July. Mid-season crops ripen from late July. Late season from approximately mid-August, continuing until mid-late September.

Berkeley NHB

Very large, sweet berry with a pale bloom. Mid-late season. Very vigorous with widely spaced stout branches. A little difficult to manage in a small garden.

Bluecrop NHB

The most popular commercial variety worldwide because of its reliability and its heavy crops of large full flavoured berries. Ripens mid-late season. It produces very long canes that need to be "topped" in order to keep bushes compact.

Bluegold NHB

Sometimes referred to as "the mortgage lifter" in Oregon as it is reliably productive, with heavy crops of well flavoured sweet fruit, with an attractive pale blue bloom. Mid-late season. Compact as a young plant, more vigorous as it ages.

Bluejay
NHB

Medium sized, firm fruit of moderate flavour. Easy to grow and crops reliably.

Bluetta
HH

Heavy crops of sweet flavoured medium sized fruit. Early. Compact. Brilliant autumn colour, attractive bronze young growth. Prone to rust infection if allowed to dry out in late summer.

Brigitta
NHB

Large crops of large firm berries. Late. Good flavour and excellent storage – keeping in a refrigerator for eight weeks or more if required. Good tempered to grow and more resistant to drought than most.

Chandler
NHB

Enormous well flavoured fruit with firm flesh, can be produced from this mid-late ripening variety. Reliable and heavy cropping. Bushes are vigorous with sturdy branches, easy to control by pruning.

Chippewa
HH

Upright, slightly spreading. Good sized berries, regularly productive and reliable. Mid-season.

Coville
NHB

Firm fleshed, large berries. Late season. Tart until fully ripe and may not ripen at all in colder regions. Bushes are moderately vigorous.

Darrow
NHB

Large to very large berries, highly flavoured and slightly aromatic. Late ripening. Vigorous spreading bushes.

Dixi
NHB

Medium to large, dark blue berries with excellent aromatic flavour. Rarely grown now as it is very late ripening and bushes are very vigorous with a spreading habit.

Duke
NHB

One of the first to ripen, but flowers quite late, acting as a useful pollinator for many other varieties in the garden. Reliable cropper with medium to large sweet berries. Growth is stocky and does not branch freely without pruning.

Earliblue
NHB

Large berries, sweet, but needing plenty of sun to bring out the flavour. Early. Growth is vigorous, producing very long canes that need pruning to keep height under control.

Elizabeth
NHB

Medium to large sweet berries ripening over a long period from mid-season. Bushes are vigorous and spreading.

Elliott
NHB

Heavy crops of medium sized berries that ripen very late. Flavour is good when fruit is fully ripe.

Herbert
NHB

Although not regarded as visually attractive, with little "bloom", this variety is mainly appreciated for its very large superior flavoured berries. Bushes have pale green leaves and are not as tall as most highbush varieties.

Ivanhoe
NHB

Large round berries with excellent, highly aromatic flavour. Bushes upright, strong and vigorous, reaching more than 2 meters. Needs pruning to the ground every few years.

Jersey
NHB

Medium sized berries, lacking in flavour. Late ripening. Bushes are very vigorous and difficult to control.

Legacy
SHB

Heavy crops of medium sized light blue berries, produced mid-late season. Excellent,sweet flavour. Bushes are vigorous and shapely, attractive especially in spring when the pale cream flower buds contrast well with the magenta winter foliage. Good in containers in southern areas, or in sheltered gardens elsewhere.

Misty
SHB

Large, light blue berries. Flavour is good. Growth is upright, vigorous with attractive grey-green foliage in summer, magenta in winter. May produce excessive crops that need thinning as soon as berries form to prevent too much stress on the plant.

Northblue
HH

Very large, dark blue, sweet berries. Early. Bushes are low and spreading. Flowers early and may need frost protection.

North country
HH

Small berries, similar in size and flavour to the wild American lowbush blueberries, freely produced on a low spreading bush. Very hardy but flowers early in warmer areas. Particularly attractive in a low trough.

Northsky
HH

Similar to Northcountry but more upright and compact.

O'Neal
SHB

Large fruit, good flavour. Early. Bushes are open, upright, vigorous and productive. Hardier than many Southern highbush hybrids.

Ozarkblue
SHB

Large, light blue berries, good sweet flavour. Crops reliably and heavily, mid-late season. Bushes are upright and vigorous with fine twiggy growth.

Patriot
NHB

Large berries of superior flavour, reliably produced as a "second early" variety. Bushes are upright and very hardy. Slightly more tolerant of marginally poorly drained soil conditions than most.

Polaris
HH

Often paired with Chippewa, but taller, more compact and upright. Must have another variety for pollination. Berries are medium sized of excellent flavour, early.

Putte

A selection from a colony of wild lowbush blueberries, obtained from a Nova Scotia breeding programme and selected and named in Sweden. Plants have a neat bushy habit, grow to 30 to 45cm and produce heavy crops of small, sweet, blue-black berries typical of the wild species. It has survived -40°C in central Sweden. May 30th, unripe fruit.

Spartan
NHB

Large berries, excellent flavour, second early. Moderately productive. Bushes upright, open and very hardy.

Sunshine Blue
SHB

Medium sized light blue berries, good flavour when fully ripe. Self fertile. Very heavy, bright pink flower bud set, usually needing thinning to avoid overtaxing plants. Mid-late season ripening, often still picking until the first frosts. Bushes are compact, evergreen, with blue-green leaves, very attractive in containers.

Tophat
HH

Very dwarf, rarely reaching more than 30cm. Medium sized berries, about 75gm per bush. Rather critical in its requirements and regarded as difficult to grow by most gardeners. Very ornamental with brilliant autumn colour.

Toro
NHB

Large berries, good flavour, high yielding and ripening mid-season in a concentrated period. Bushes are upright, stocky and fairly vigorous.

Chapter 8. Propagation

Blueberries have, traditionally, been propagated from stem cuttings. These are either taken in summer as semi-hardwood cuttings or as hardwood cuttings, taken in winter. They are not the easiest plants to root by either method.

Many nurseries now use micropropagation (tissue culture) if they need to produce large quantities of blueberry plants.

Semi-hardwood cuttings

Short lateral stems of the current year's growth and of about 10cm (4 inches) length, are removed, preferably with a "heel", once the stems are firm, no longer "floppy" at the tip. This is usually in June or early July, but depends on the variety and the particular season.

The lower leaf/leaves are removed in order to allow sufficient leafless stem to be inserted in the rooting medium, and the cut end is dipped in rooting hormone. The prepared cutting is inserted in a rooting medium which has traditionally been 50% peat : 50% perlite or sharp sand, and watered in. 100% humidity is essential, by using a mist unit in a propagator or a polythene "tent".

Shade will be needed during the summer months to prevent overheating under the polythene.

Provided the cuttings remain turgid and are not overheated they should form roots before the cold weather arrives. They should be left unpotted and unfed until the following spring.

Hardwood cuttings

A frost free greenhouse, with background heat available in severe weather, is required for success with this method.

Cuttings are taken from healthy canes from the previous year's growth, towards the end of winter but before buds start to swell.

10-12cm lengths are cut from canes of about a pencil's diameter, making sure there are three or four viable buds on each length, and avoiding the top few centimeters of the cane.

A healthy blueberry plant, already showing strong growth from the buds on a hardwood cutting, with roots pushing out through a biodegradable cell

The lowest ends of the canes are dipped in rooting hormone and the cuttings inserted in a rooting medium as before.

Once again 100% humidity is needed around the cuttings and, at this time of year, bottom heat at about 19ºC.

Leaves grow first, using the energy from starch stored under the bark. (See page 26). They, of course, need 100% humidity as there are no roots at this stage to provide water from below. Good light, but not direct sunlight, helps the efficiency of the leaves. Some shade may be needed in sunny spells.

A few weeks later a callus forms at the base of the cutting and it is from this that roots emerge, usually some time in late spring. The root system grows rapidly, forming a fibrous mass. This is easily broken from the stem, so great care is needed when potting up. Degradable peat or paper compound cells are often used as these can later be potted up in their entirety, reducing the risk of damage considerably.

Once firmly rooted and starting to show shoot growth the young plants should be potted up, using an ericaceous compost, into small pots and given a little protection in a cold frame until they are well established.

Blueberry plants grow very fast in the first year and produce long canes even at this age. These should be pinched out to encourage branching.

Young blueberry plants from semi-hardwood cuttings – from hardwood cuttings.

Chapter 9. Problems, pests and diseases

There are relatively few pests and diseases experienced by gardeners growing blueberry plants at home.

Some of the problems experienced are connected to the cultivation methods used.

Some **Frequently Asked Questions**, based on actual correspondence :-

Q. Some of my young blueberry plants are flowering and fruiting others are not.

A. Varieties vary. Some crop at an early age, often at the expense of growth. Others naturally spend energy on producing shoots instead, and incidentally produce better crops sooner.

Q. I have one blueberry plant and it has never fruited. It has flowers but never any berries.

A. It is evidently not a self fertile variety and needs a second variety nearby in order for the bees to pollinate and fertilise its flowers.

Q. One of my blueberry plants looks sick, but it has a healthy shoot growing from its base. This has never produced berries.

A. This is a "cuckoo in the nest" situation. A willow seedling has developed in the pot and, having great vigour, is taking over. Willow seedlings have greener stems than blueberries and smaller, darker leaves in spring.

Q. My blueberry plants, bought three years ago and potted according to instructions, are not growing. I feed them with "Sequestrene".

A. This product, which contains sequestered iron, supplies iron, which is just one of the minor elements needed. It is useful in marginally alkaline conditions when the alkalinity chemically "locks up" necessary minerals, as it helps to set them free. It does not, however, supply necessary nitrogen, phosphorus, potash etc.

The willow seedling, on the right, may be confused with the blueberry plant, especially in winter

Q. My blueberry plants have been potted into fresh compost and I have also fed them, with an ericaceous fertiliser, to "get them going". They seem to have white stuff round all the leaf margins.

A. This is the plants' way of disposing of excess minerals. Flush their soil through with clear water to remove this excess.

Q. The leaves on my plants have all gone dark green with brown edges. They have grown very vigorously. I feed them with my tomatoes.

A. Indigestion! Too much of the wrong diet. (See "Feeding" page 32).

Q. Should I cut my blueberry plants back every year, or "tip" the young shoots ?

A. No! See "Pruning", page 32.

Q. I bought three blueberry plants in February and, as it was very cold, have kept them on the windowsill of our lounge. They all started to grow well. Now all the leaves are shrivelling and the plants look as if they are dying.

A. Your plants have been "killed by kindness" ! Most nurseries keep their blueberry plants in nursery beds outside all year round so they are used to low temperatures, and freezing conditions.

If worried about cold conditions in your area when the plants arrive, keep in an unheated shed or garage until it is possible to plant them.

Pests

Mammal pests such as deer, badgers and rabbits have already been mentioned when considering preparation for planting blueberries.

Netting to exclude birds has also been suggested as an essential provision.

Bigger birds like pigeons, blackbirds and thrushes not only eat the fruit but knock unripe berries to the ground and, being heavy, break new shoots

Smaller birds often peck at the berries, making an easy meal for wasps

Insect pests

Vine weevils Otiorhynchus sulcatus. These are mainly destructive in containers, with the twofold damage caused by larvae eating the bark where stems join roots at soil level and also where they demolish roots deeper down. Both can cause collapse of even quite large plants if these pests are allowed to continue. The damage to leaves, caused by the adults, is cosmetic and not significant to the plants.

The adults are long snouted brown weevils active mostly at night. Signs of their presence are semi-circular notches at the margins of young leaves.

This root system is detached & vine weevil larvae are found in the compost

They are all female – no need for males – and lay their eggs in the soil in two periods of the year. Larvae are active in spring and early summer and the second brood in September/October.

As blueberries are grown for edible berries the only safe means of control is biological. One popular and easy-to-use method involves drenching compost with a suspension of nematodes, which are found naturally in the soil but produced commercially in vast quantities. These arrive in impregnated sponges in sealed plastic boxes and have to be dispersed into clean cold water in a watering can, or knapsack sprayer with a coarse nozzle attached. The drench is then applied to wet compost and the nematodes swim in the soil water, homing in on their specific vine weevil larvae targets. To quote the literature, they "enter by any orifice", and feed, releasing a bacterium inside the larvae, which die quite quickly, leaving a concentration of nematode eggs to continue the cycle.

Chewed leaves

Blueberry fly. This is, so far, a major pest in American blueberry plantations and of little significance in the UK. The damage is caused by the larvae of a small fly. Females lay one egg under the skin of a berry just as it starts to ripen. Eggs hatch into larvae which eat away at the flesh of the berry, which turns pale, fails to develop and falls to the ground.

Cranberry fruitworm. Again, this is not yet a major pest in Britain.
The grubs that cause the damage are larvae of a small moth which burrow into the stem end of young, green berries and eat the contents from within. The first signs of an invasion may

be smaller than usual berries turning blue and failing to develop properly. Sometimes a web is constructed that enmeshes several berries. When ready the larvae fall to the ground, pupate and overwinter in the leaf litter or other debris below bushes.

Removal of all debris is usually sufficient to control this pest in the garden.

Fungal diseases

Most can be kept at bay by good cultivation – removing and burning any dead leaves and prunings that are suspected of carrying spores, or disposing of them in landfill rubbish. Also by avoiding over-generosity with fertiliser, especially late in the summer.

Grey mould *Botrytis cinerea*
This common plant disease most often affects young blueberry plants that have become "soft" for some reason and vulnerable to physical damage which opens the way for fungal spores to enter wounds or invade vulnerable tissues. Perhaps the plants had too much fertiliser too late in the growing season so that they fail to ripen the new growth, which then gets damaged by frost, which causes damaged tissues.

Shoot tips turn black and the fungus spreads down the stem. If flowers are affected, usually in whole clusters, they turn brown and stay attached instead of falling to the ground naturally, spores fall on young leaves.

Affected fruit is spoiled.

A fungal attack of Botrytis cinerea affects leaves, stems and flowers

Winter damage may cause problems by killing young stems, especially of the less hardy varieties when they may have failed to become fully dormant the previous autumn. Fungal problems frequently follow when temperatures rise in the spring. If all blackened stems are cut back and a fungicide spray used recovery is remarkably swift. Although no flowers will appear that year, by the following spring plants are likely to be of excellent quality and have flowers and fruit.

Some of the less hardy blueberry plants may be damaged and lose their flower buds in severe winter weather. Fungal diseases such as Botrytis may follow. They may need a little extra care, but generally recover well and produce a crop the following year.

(1) 'Sunshine Blue'. Initially damaged by severe frost. Botrytis rot followed. (4th May)

(2) 'Sunshine Blue' recovering a month after trimming. (1st June)

(3) A year later. It is now a good plant with a nice balance between leaves and flowers.

Blueberry Rust *Pucciniastrum vaccinii*

This has occurred in late summer, in some areas, when plants are subjected to hot dry conditions coupled with lack of water. It appears first as orange spots on the leaves, which spread to become patches. If not controlled affected leaves will fall. No lasting damage is done to the plants but they may be infected the following year if all leaf litter, from which spores can develop, are not removed. Prompt spraying should halt development. There are organic fungicides available for food producing plants. One we have trialled is Potassium bicarbonate. (Not Sodium bicarbonate, the ingredient in many remedies for indigestion !)

In America, where large areas are devoted to growing blueberries and especially where there is also a long established wild population of them, fungal diseases and insect pests can be a major problem.

Small aircraft can sometimes be seen swooping low over the larger plantations, spraying with approved fungicides to control "mummyberry", a fungus that causes shrivelled and inedible fruit.

A biological spray, containing a bacterium is also used to destroy the harmful grubs or larvae of several moths that hatch amongst the flowers and prevent fruit forming. Unlike most chemical sprays, it is completely harmless to bees.

Chapter 10. A word about cranberries

These relatives of blueberries enjoy the same soil conditions and make ideal companions in the garden.

Found growing wild in moist acidic conditions in North America the species, *Vaccinium macrocarpon*, has larger berries and is a little less hardy than the native European cranberry, *Vaccinium oxycoccus*, which is quite rare in Britain and found mostly in boggy northern upland areas.

The North American cranberry tends to live through summer in drier conditions, although commercial cranberry growers do use overhead sprinklers to irrigate some "bogs".

North American wild cranberries have been picked for centuries by the native people and dried in the sun or over the smoke from their fires, ready for storage and use in winter cooking pots.

Cranberries are also used as an ingredient of pemmican. This was made by combining finely cut meat, often from the caribou deer, with whatever wild fruits were available. These ingredients were bound together with fat. Cakes of pemmican were a staple food of hunters and fishermen on their expeditions as they were easily carried, needed no cooking pot and provided a high energy food.

My own attempts at making pemmican at home resulted in cakes that have lasted three years in a box in my dry store cupboard without evident deterioration. I haven't quite dared to eat them !

Cranberries have been grown commercially in North America for much longer than blueberries, having attracted the attention of European settlers in the 18th century. These people originally followed the example of the native Americans and picked the fruit from wild plants. They later dug up clumps from favoured areas and grew them in a more controlled manner in fields, just like any other crop. They thrived in sandy soil where fresh water was available for growth in summer.

For a long time the berries were harvested by hand; a tedious and back-breaking business. Later, in 1925, a motor driven, hand steered harvesting machine was invented. More recent designs based on this type are still used to harvest berries from small acreages today. These machines look a little like garden lawn mowers, but instead of blades they have combs that scoop the berries from the vines. Unfortunately a significant percentage of the crop remains at the base of the plants and on the ground and much of that harvested is bruised and suitable only for processing into sauces or juice.

Cranberry field just after it has been "dry harvested"   *Cranberry fruit halved to show air pockets*

It is a popular belief that cranberries are grown in water. This is not surprising as people talk about "Cranberry bogs" and the pictures that are published show acres of red berries floating on water at harvest time in autumn.

Water is actually used as a "tool" to aid harvesting the crop. Cranberries are filled with air and are able to act as floats to carry the slender vines up in the water. Having delicate stalks, the fruit is quite easily detached if there is enough fresh water to allow this to happen. This method provides a significant improvement in yields, as a much higher percentage of the berries are gathered undamaged.

At harvest time, from September to late October, teams of men wearing waders and guiding hand held machines can be seen at work in flooded "bogs". Berries float to the surface where they can be guided to elevators and taken to the pack-houses in lorries. Here they have all the dross removed and the fruit is packed into polythene bags and sold for use, mostly in sauces, to accompany the turkey for Thanksgiving and Christmas dinners. In the larger cranberry producing farms huge harvesting machines are used.

Harvesting in full swing in a New Jersey cranberry bog. Late October.

At home, gardeners can of course enjoy their own cranberry crops.. Some people plant beds of 20 or more cranberry plants and harvest plenty of berries to use in traditional cranberry sauce. In addition to the traditional uses a few cranberries thrown into a stewpot, particularly of venison or other game, bring out all sorts of excellent flavours. Cranberry and cheese scones are delicious too.

The plants, if put into the ground about 30-40cm apart, will quickly form a mat as the runners produced each summer root into the soil as they grow, rather like strawberry runners.

They start to produce a little fruit from 2-3 years of age after propagation and gradually increase in yield each year. When the vines start to become too matted and woody, producing less and less fruit, they need to be rejuvenated.

Commercial growers mow them down in winter. Gardeners use shears or secateurs. There will of course be no crop the following year, but the plants grow quickly and two or possibly three years after cutting down good crops can be expected again.

This ten year old bed in a large kitchen garden in Ireland is mown every few years to remove tired old "vines" and to encourage new growth.

Many people put cranberries around their blueberry plants, in the garden, in raised beds, or in tubs, using the space to the maximum by enjoying two crops instead of just one, and an enhanced ornamental feature too.

Berries ripen in September or early October, but can remain on the vines until the following February or March. This year I picked my last cranberry in May. Birds are no problem and both mice and squirrels seem generally uninterested.

Some gardeners even grow cranberries in hanging baskets, not only to produce berries for the kitchen but also as an attractive and unusual ornamental feature. A 14 inch basket will need three or four small cranberry plants to fill it.

Cranberries need little care. However cranberry plants, as most plants with roots severely restricted, in hanging baskets, small pots, window boxes and other relatively small containers, do need more attention paid to watering than those in the garden or raised beds. Water retaining gels are a real help here.

If planted in the garden in acidic soil with plenty of well rotted woody material cranberries will not need feeding. If in containers they need a little ericaceous fertiliser. Just a pinch of slow release pellets per plant (or per 3 in a hanging basket) is enough.

Cranberry vines trailing over the edge of a half beer barrel containing a blueberry plant in full autumn colour

Weed control is necessary, removing weeds as soon as they appear, as it is much more difficult to extricate them from a mat of cranberry plants later.

Pruning of cranberry plants in containers is a slightly more exact science than in outdoor beds. Each plant is treated as an individual. Annual winter cutting back of the longest trailing "vines" (runners), to an area where there is branching, will encourage more future growth of the "uprights" on the main plants. These short stems will bear fruit in future, drooping to a horizontal position as the fruit ripens, and becoming runners in the following summer.

Propagation is very easy; in America, commercial cranberry growers spread sand over their "bogs" and cut long vines into approximately 10cm pieces. These are then inserted roughly into the ground using disc harrows attached to a tractor. In the garden similar sized pieces cut from trailing vines, once the growth has become firm at the tip, in late summer, are inserted

This hanging basket has enough fruit for the sauce to accompany the turkey

into a sand/peat mix in pots and kept outside. They usually form roots within a month. No need for a propagating frame or any other complicated facility.

Ripe cranberries on their slender stalks

Although quite hardy, it is asking too much to keep cranberries suspended in freezing air so it is recommended that hanging baskets are lowered, or even kept in a shed or unheated greenhouse, during periods of severe weather.

As can be seen, cranberries make very attractive plants in winter. The bright red berries often stay on the vines until spring, if not picked, and the magenta leaves set them off well, especially when lightly frosted.

In mid-summer there is the added bonus of delicate pink flowers. The long protruding pistils, with the recurving petals, apparently reminded some of the early settlers, who landed on the east coastal marshes of America, of the Marsh Crane bird. The name "Craneberry" is said to come from this story.

Varieties

There are many varieties available for those who seek a choice. The following is a small selection.

'Early Black'. A wild selection producing good crops of small to medium slightly pear shaped berries that turn very dark red when fully ripe. They ripen as early as the beginning of September in southern England but store well in a refrigerator.
This is an attractive, easy-to-grow variety for gardeners. In summer it has light green leaves, but these turn deep red in winter. 'Early Black' is very hardy and is tolerant of slightly less acidic soils than most varieties.

'Franklin'. A cross between 'Early Black' and 'Howes', it ripens just after 'Early Black' and can produce more fruit than its parents, but takes longer to establish as its vines are not quite so vigorous. Berries are of medium to large size, round and red to dark red.
This is a good variety to plant in gardens with little space available as it is naturally more compact than most cranberries.

'Early Black'

'Howes'. A wild selection made in 1843, and still sold today as it is vigorous, frost resistant and quick to establish. It's vigour can be a problem for the tidy-minded however as vines easily become tangled. The fruit ripens late, sometimes into mid-October in southern England, is of small to medium size, round and an attractive glossy red.

'Pilgrim'. This variety has particularly large purplish red berries with a waxy bloom and creamy coloured flesh. It takes a little time

'Pilgrim'

to grow but once established it is capable of heavy crops. Although not the most ornamental variety it is definitely one for fruit production for Christmas as it ripens late.

'Stevens'. The large round berries, flattened at both ends, are an attractive deep red and glossy. They ripen mid-season and store well. This variety is easy to grow, vigorous and productive from a young age.

'Stevens'

Pests and diseases

In the main cranberry growing areas of Canada and North America significant numbers of pests have built up over the years. The damage is mostly caused by the larvae of a variety of moths and weevils. So far, in Europe there is no concentration of cranberry growing. Any small infestation seen in a garden is easily dealt with by being observant and removing, by hand, any grubs found amongst the blossom or berries.

The main insect pest that affects cranberry plants in gardens is the black vine weevil, '*Otiorhynchus sulcatus*'. Plants that suddenly collapse as growth starts in Spring or as the growing season nears its end in late summer are usually found to have virtually no roots. They have been eaten away by the larvae of this common garden pest. Effective control is by using parasitic nematodes in a drench.
See page 62.

Diseases are also relatively insignificant in Europe. Root rot can cause death especially if container grown plants have water-logged roots in summer. Healthy roots need oxygen but the fungus thrives in warm airless conditions so good summer drainage is needed to prevent this disease.

A variety of fungal rots may affect stems, flowers and later the fruit. They usually occur when plants are over-fed and too "soft".

John Webb known as 'Peg Leg John', a cranberry grower from New Jersey, with only one sound leg, unwittingly discovered a method for identifying diseased or damaged cranberries. To save carrying trays down his stairs from the storage loft to his packhouse he resorted to pouring the fruit down the stairs. The healthy, firm berries bounced down while the unsound ones failed to bounce and reach the bottom. The "bouncing" principle is used in grading machines to this day.

Chapter 11. Lingonberries

Lingonberry flowers and fruit at various stages of ripening at the end of August

These plants, *Vaccinium vitis-idaea,* related to blueberries and cranberries, are found growing wild in the cold climates of Northern Europe, particularly in Sweden and Germany, and also rarely in northern Britain.

The berry is sometimes known as the partridgeberry, cowberry, foxberry or wolfberry and, in Scandinavia as tyttebaer.

Plants grow in very poor acidic, dry sandy soil and for those who have pine trees in the garden they are of particular benefit, giving an ideal ground cover. They provide a glossy evergreen carpet where little else will grow.

Growing to about 20-30cm in height, they can be planted about 20cm apart and used as a low hedge as an alternative to Box (Buxus), beside a path or to surround a planted bed of, say, cranberries.

Alternatively they make an unusual feature in a container, either on their own or planted around a blueberry bush.

The flowers are small and of a delicate pink, making an attractive contrast with the glossy foliage.

Normally, lingonberries have two flowering periods, May-June and August-September.

The small bright red glossy berries follow in July-August and, if autumn does not come too early, in October-November. As with cranberries, birds and other predators tend to leave them alone as they are acidic and "sharp" to eat uncooked.

They are relatively new to cultivation in the garden, but so far the main lessons learned are that they do not like to have wet roots in winter and they are happy is shade or in sun.

If grown in containers they need only a small amount of ericaceous fertiliser, sprinkled over the soil around them, in spring. In the garden rotted pine needles, both incorporated ahead of planting and used as mulch seem to give good results with no need for annual feeding.

From spring onwards lingonberries send out short runners which soon develop upright shoots to spread the plants laterally. These grow close to the parent plants so quite dense clumps are formed and lateral spread is relatively slow.

Propagation is either by division, as the plants send down roots from each lateral growth, or by rooting individual shoots in sand or a 50:50 peat:sand mix.

Varieties

Mature plants of some of the new cultivated varieties can produce up to 1Kg of fruit per plant per year, but yields tend to be around 500g in the garden.

'Koralle'. This is the most well known variety. Originally produced in Holland as an ornamental ground-cover plant it has subsequently been taken up by commercial growers for production of its fruit.

Koralle has light red glossy berries that are produced on plants from about three years of age. It has a bushy habit and spreads laterally relatively slowly. It is fussy about soil conditions and will not thrive in even slightly alkaline soils or in wet situations.

'Red Pearl'. A compact but fast spreading variety with bright red berries and highly ornamental bronze young growth contrasting well with the glossy dark green older leaves and visible all summer. It is less demanding than 'Koralle', growing in less than ideal soil conditions. 'Red Pearl' regularly has two flowering periods in all but the coldest climates. Flowers and fruit can appear together until late in the autumn.

The berries have similar eating qualities to cranberries but with a little more intense flavour, being quite sharp and needing some sugar to sweeten. They are regarded in some circles as a fruit for connoisseurs as they take time and effort to pick in the wild.

Commercial cultivation is, to date, only carried out on a small scale in the USA.

Lingonberry compote is a favourite product in Scandinavia and can be bought in many stores owned by a well known Scandinavian furniture company in several European countries. It is a delicious and unusual accompaniment for cold meats and cheeses, much favoured at breakfast. The berries can, like cranberries, also be used in casseroles.

Lingonberry flowers

Chapter 12.
Full circle: The Whitesbog Blueberry Festival

Every year in late June, when the blueberry harvest is coming to an end in the Pine Barrens area of New Jersey, the Whitesbog Blueberry Festival is held. It is organised by the Whitesbog Trust, a group of enthusiasts who realise the international significance of the place as the home of the beginning of a world-wide industry, and aim to not only preserve it but to keep it active and available to the general public.

The annual event is partly a secular "harvest festival" and partly a reminder of the work of Elizabeth White whose home was at Whitesbog. Her house, Sunningive, is open for visitors and some of the buildings in the previously neglected village have been restored, including the village shop. Barns house a museum exhibiting some of the equipment used by the Whites and their staff on the very extensive cranberry bogs and less extensive blueberry plantations. One of the aluminium gauges supplied to the old "pineys" when they were sent out to select the original wild blueberry plants is also on show.

During the festival there are tractor-trailer rides around the farm, accompanied by "Dr Coville" who tells the story of the great man's work and achievements. "Elizabeth White" takes tours round Sunningive and there are talks and film shows in some of the other buildings so there is every opportunity to learn about the early introduction of the blueberry as a commercial crop.

Outside a Bluegrass Band plays and there are stalls selling all manner of blueberry products.

The highlight of the afternoon is the "Blueberry Pie Eating Competition", when children compete to see who can eat a slice of blueberry pie in the fastest time. This is when the TV and local press cameras, together with a host of family photographers, crowd round the long tables in the centre of the festival site.

The festival is a happy and enjoyable celebration of America's favourite berry and a reminder of where its cultivation all started.

Elizabeth White was not only a pioneer of blueberry cultivation but she thought about their marketing. A gift of a box of chocolates from Paris led to what is now standard practice in many fruit pack-houses. Her chocolates were covered by a cellophane lid, so she traced the manufacturers in France, ordered the materials from them and presented her blueberries for sale in boxes with cellophane lids. A quite unique idea at the time.

Children, with hands behind their backs, competing in the blueberry pie eating competition

A variety of cakes and other goodies on sale at this stall

The winner, Nick Wells, with a triumphant and very engaging "blueberry smile" !

Food for thought.....

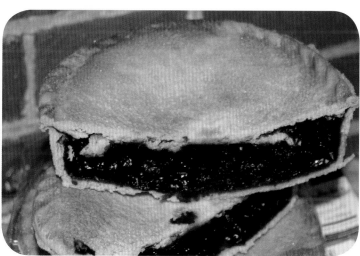

Acknowledgements

David Trehane

In writing this book I have always been conscious of the tremendous inspiration and influence provided by my late father, David Trehane. It was his pioneering spirit that not only brought blueberries to Britain, but also started them on the road to popularity by having the courage to plant sufficient numbers to provide the first commercial crops.

I owe him thanks also for asking me to help found the family nursery, where I learned much about propagating and growing blueberries.

Travels to other countries added more knowledge and photographs.

Thanks to :

The Wild Blueberry Association of North America, based at Bar Harbour in Maine and the Allen family, wild blueberry growers, also in Maine.

Gary Pavlis and Mark Ehlenfeldt from the USDA in New Jersey.

The Whitesbog Preservation Trust for the use of the picture of Elizabeth White and Dr Coville on page 13, and also many folk at Whitesbog, New Jersey, including young Nick Wells and his family.

Wilhelm and Sonja Dierking from the Dierking Nursery, Germany, for inspiration, guidance and access for photography.

Staff at Fall Creek Nursery in Oregon for allowing me to take many pictures of the huge range of blueberry varieties produced there.

Staff at BFA (Blueberry Farms of Australia), at Corindi, NSW, for useful information about growing blueberries in hot climates.

My sister Julia has been invaluable as a proof reader. Many thanks to her.

Lastly, many thanks to Graham Mallett of GPM Computer Services, Colehill, Wimborne for his invaluable work and great patience in helping me to design this book and for doing the layout in preparation for printing.